BGI

FAITH IN FRIENDSHIP

My Friend Is
Jewish

by Laya Saul

PURPLE TOAD
PUBLISHING

My Friend Is Buddhist
My Friend Is Christian
My Friend Is Hindu
My Friend Is Jewish
My Friend Is Muslim

PUBLISHER'S NOTE: The data in this book has been researched in depth, and to the best of our knowledge is factual. Although every measure is taken to give an accurate account, Purple Toad Publishing makes no warranty of the accuracy of the information and is not liable for damages caused by inaccuracies.

Printing 1 2 3 4 5 6 7 8 9

Publisher's Cataloging-in-Publication Data
Saul, Laya
   Faith in friendship : my friend is Jewish / Laya Saul
      p. cm.
Includes bibliographic references and index.
ISBN: 9781624691065
1. Judaism – History – Juvenile literature. 2. Judaism – Traditions – Juvenile literature.   I. Title.
 BM 650
 296S
                                                    2014941902

eBook ISBN: 9781624691072

Contents

Chapter One: Danny Meets the Twins 5

    Jewish Time 9

Chapter Two: Twelve Tribes, One Vibe 11

    One Simple Prayer 17

Chapter Three: Living as a Jew 19

    What is a Jew? 25

Chapter Four: From Generation to Generation 27

    What's in a Name? 33

Chapter Five: Standing as One—Judaism Today 35

    One Light 41

Timeline 42

Further Reading 43

    Books 43

    Works Consulted 44

    On the Internet 45

Glossary 46

Index 47

Our class listens.

Danny Meets the Twins

"Tell me, Jew," the commanding soldier's muscles bulged as his hand gripped his sword, "tell me what it means to live as a Jew." He sneered and added, "And tell me while you stand on one leg!"

All the kids in class seemed to hold their breath as they listened to hear how the story would unfold.

I glanced over at Danny, our neighbor who was visiting me and my twin sister, Ora, for the day. He sat on the edge of his seat. Though not Jewish himself, Danny was interested to learn more about the Jewish day school we attended.

My name is Yehuda. When we moved into our apartment complex, Danny couldn't wait to knock on the door and introduce himself. Danny's great grandfather fought in the US army against the Germans in World War II. He was one of the first soldiers to help free Jewish people from Nazi camps. Danny had heard the stories and had

Yahuda (left) and Danny quickly discovered they loved the same things, like baseball, Star Wars, and building incredible cities in Minecraft on their computers.

even seen pictures his great grandfather had taken, but he didn't really know who the Jewish people were. He was excited to learn more and asked a lot of questions. At school with us, he listened to what would happen in this story.

The teacher continued, "Rabbi Hillel answered the officer, '"Do not do to others what is hateful to you. The rest is commentary. Now go learn.'" Danny nodded as the class continued the discussion of what that meant exactly. Then they talked about unity, what it is and why it is important. They sang a Hebrew song, *"Hee'nay ma tov u'mah na'eem* (Here is what is good and pleasant, to sit as brothers and sisters together) . . ."

After school our mom picked us up.

"Hurry up and get in the car," mom said in an excited voice. "There's still work to prepare for *Shabbat*."

"Mom, can Danny join us for Shabbat dinner tonight?" I asked. I love celebrating Shabbat—the Sabbath day of rest. I love the special foods and rituals.

"Yeah, Mom, can he?" Ora loves lighting the candles and singing songs at the special Shabbat dinner table with our family.

Danny lives two doors down from us and hangs out at our house sometimes. He goes to the local public school and we go to a special school for Jewish studies. We eat some of the same foods but in our family we eat things Danny's never heard of. We all speak English but Ora and I also learn Hebrew in school, and that is the language we use for our prayers. We are a Jewish family who observes Jewish law and teachings according to the way it was written in the Hebrew Bible.

The main teaching of the Jews is that there is one God who created the world. We learn that God recreates the whole world in every moment. God created humankind in His image so each person has a spark of the Divine within. Danny asks me and Ora tons of questions and it is interesting for us to think about some of the things we just do automatically. I'll tell more about that in a little while.

That evening, Ora stood with our mother and sister as they lit the Shabbat candles in our home in the Rocky Mountains of Colorado. Our mother lights seven candles, one each for her and our father plus one for each of the five kids. She says that like each candle, every child brings more light into the family and the world. She circles the candlelight with her hands three times to bring the Shabbat light in, covers her eyes, and whispers the blessing for this sacred light and

Our seven candles

Chapter 1

Synagogues can be beautiful like the one in this picture but they can also be very simple and modest.

time. When she uncovers her eyes, she kisses each of the children.

Then, all dressed up in our nicest clothes, we walk to the synagogue with our father and older brothers. On the Sabbath and most holidays, observant Jews do not drive cars, turn electricity on and off, or cook. At first, this might sound like you can't do anything at all—no TV, telephones, or computers. But really it's a kind of freedom to step away from everyday worries, and to celebrate and spend time with family, and to thank God. Our mother says it's like Thanksgiving every week! At synagogue, we pray and sing to welcome in the Sabbath.

After synagogue, we come home to a beautiful dinner table, set with a white tablecloth and special braided bread called *challah*. The family sits together, sings a song to the angels, and one to our mother. Next, our father says a blessing over a cup of wine. The silver cup he uses shows how precious it is to us to make the Sabbath holy.

Then, each child, from the oldest to the youngest, stands to receive a blessing. One at a time, our father and mother softly put their hands on each of our heads. "May God bless you and protect you. May the Divine One shine His presence and grace upon you. May He turn His face to you, and may He grant you peace."

Before we eat, there is a blessing over the bread, and the family enjoys the yummy food we prepared as stories are told and teachings shared.

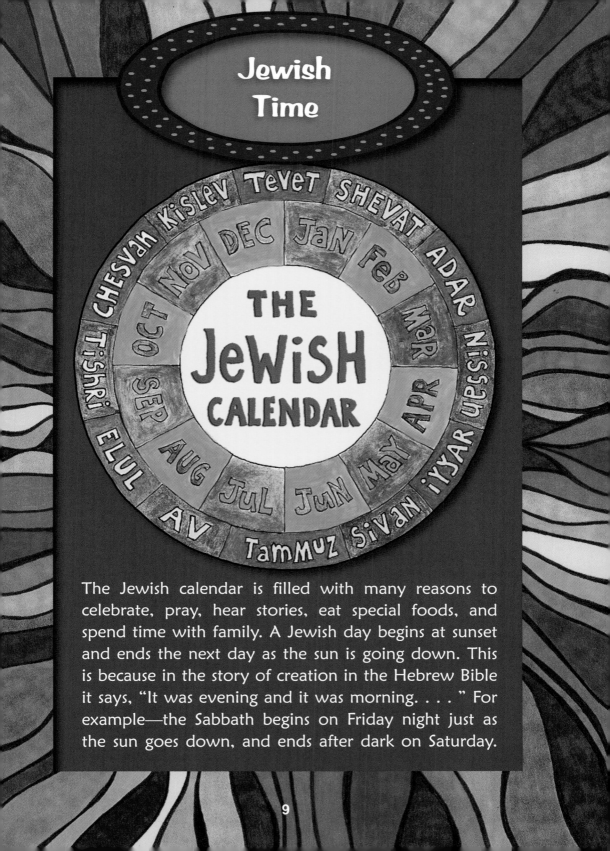

THE JEWISH CALENDAR

The Jewish calendar is filled with many reasons to celebrate, pray, hear stories, eat special foods, and spend time with family. A Jewish day begins at sunset and ends the next day as the sun is going down. This is because in the story of creation in the Hebrew Bible it says, "It was evening and it was morning. . . ." For example—the Sabbath begins on Friday night just as the sun goes down, and ends after dark on Saturday.

Shavuot
cheesecake

Twelve Tribes, One Vibe

Cheesecake!!! Everyone in our family is excited because our mother is making cheesecake for the holiday of Shavuot (shah-vu-AHT). Every spring, exactly seven weeks after the Passover holiday that celebrates freedom from slavery in Egypt thousands of years ago, the Jews celebrate the giving of the Torah—the Hebrew Bible (also known as the Five Books of Moses; Christians call it the Old Testament) at Mount Sinai.

Ora loves to tell stories, so she told Danny all about the beginnings of the Jewish nation.

Thousands of years ago, after many miracles and wonders, the Jews were freed from a harsh slavery in Egypt. The Jews, led by Moses, traveled in the Sinai desert until they reached Mount Sinai. It was there that God spoke to the Jews as a nation. In other religions, it is believed that one man had the revelation (when God revealed Himself). But at Mount Sinai *all* the Jews—men, women, and children—heard God's voice

Travelers visit what is thought to be Mount Sinai. Mount Sinai was the place that the Jewish Nation heard God's voice giving them the Ten Commandments. It was the place they received the Torah, the sacred teachings of how to be close to God and bring Godliness into the world.

together! What did God say? He said, "I am the Lord your God who took you out of Egypt." It may *sound* simple but it is said that it was such a powerful moment that the souls of every person there were blown out of their bodies and that God had to put them back! That is true awe. He gave the Jews the Ten Commandments as they stood at the base of that small mountain. That is called "national revelation." The teachings God gave the Jews on that day have been passed down from generation to generation for thousands of years. In fact, the very word *Torah* comes from the Hebrew word meaning "to teach."

The story of the Jews and Judaism begins before that with a little boy named Abraham. His father made idols—statues that people could pray to. The people who bought the idols believed that they were actual gods. But Abraham realized there had to be something more. How could someone pray to a statue that was only a few hours old and only yesterday had been just a lump of wood or clay? One story about Abraham tells of the ruler of the time, Nimrod, who thought himself a god. The cruel man threw young Abraham into a fiery furnace when he heard that Abraham was destroying idols. Miraculously, Abraham was not burned. He later earned the name Abraham the Hebrew.

The Torah tells about Abraham's journey together with his wife Sarah. God sent them to the Land of Israel and promised Abraham that a nation would come from him. Abraham had two sons. Ishmael was his first son. Ishmael's mother was named Hagar. From Ishmael descended the nation of Islam. It was Abraham's younger son, Isaac, whose mother was Sarah, who built the nation of the Jews. Isaac and his wife Rebecca also had two sons—Esau and Jacob. From Esau came the ancient nation of Rome and from Jacob came the twelve tribes of Israel—the Jewish nation—one tribe from each of Jacob's sons.

"Guess what!" Ora said to Danny. "Yehuda was one of those twelve sons! Isn't it amazing that my brother's name has been around for so long? He was named after our grandfather, but maybe the name comes all the way from the original Yehuda."

"Whoa!" Danny said. "It's really something to have a connection to the past like that!"

Ora continued telling Danny the story of the birth of the Jewish nation.

It was Jacob's family that went down into Egypt during a famine, a time when there was no food for the people of the land. In Egypt, the sons of Jacob flourished. One of his sons even rose to great power. But after Jacob's original sons—the leaders of the twelve tribes—had all died, Pharaoh, the ruler of ancient Egypt, thought that the Hebrews (Jews of ancient times were called Hebrews or Israelites) might some day turn against him. Pharaoh made the Hebrews his slaves. It was a dark and bitter time in Jewish history. Pharaoh even decreed that every Jewish baby boy be drowned in the Nile River.

A little Hebrew slave girl named Miriam took her baby brother and put him in a floating basket in the waters of the Nile. She watched the basket float in the water. The princess of Egypt found the basket, named the baby

Moses, and adopted the infant to be raised as her son, a prince of Egypt. Miriam ran to the princess and asked if she wanted a nursemaid for the infant. When the princess said yes, Miriam ran to get her mother.

Moses knew who he really was. One day he saw an Egyptian guard beating a Hebrew. Moses killed the guard and ran away from Egypt into the desert. In the desert, he saw a bush that was on fire but it wasn't burning up. There he heard God's voice. "Go back to Egypt and tell Pharaoh to let My people go." At first, Moses was not so sure he was the man for the job and he even argued with God. God told Moses that his brother Aaron would also stand with him.

"When we celebrate the holiday of Passover," Ora continued, "we tell the story of Pharaoh and how he oppressed the Jews even more after Moses told him to let the Hebrews go. Then real miracles started to happen. God brought ten plagues down onto the Egyptians. Water turned to blood, frogs overran Egypt, swarms and swarms of locusts came and ravaged the crops. There was so much drama that there have even been movies made about this story.

Moses and the Burning Bush by Sebastien Bourdon

"The Hebrews escaped Egypt and the miracles followed them. God split the sea for them when Pharaoh and his army cornered them. Then, a special food called *manna* came from Heaven each day like the morning dew to feed them.

"Well, that catches you up," I chimed in. "After the Hebrews left Egypt, they went to Mount Sinai in the desert and were given the Ten Commandments."

"So what's the big deal about cheesecake?" Danny asked. "What's the connection between cheesecake and the Bible?"

"When the Jews received the whole Torah, they also received the Biblical laws of what to eat and what not to

The Destruction of Pharaoh's Host by John Martin, 1833, shows the Red Sea filling back in to destroy Pharaoh's army.

eat. Those dietary laws are called *kashrut,* or in English, "kosher." Since there are so many restrictions on the kinds of animals Jews can eat, the nation stuck to dairy for a while," I smiled.

Now Danny wanted to know more. "How could such a small nation be around for so long? What kept them alive in a world where all the major powers throughout history have fallen?

"And what did the Jews do after they received the Torah at Mount Sinai?" He asked.

I continued the story as Ora got us all cookies and drinks. "The Jews headed back to the Promised Land, the land that God promised to Abraham. Along the way there were nations that were not so happy to see them. Armies attacked them and one king even hired a powerful sorcerer to try to curse them."

"There are sorcerers in the Torah?" Danny asked, amazed.

"Yes!" I nodded. "The sorcerer's name was Bilaam and he was very powerful. But God is above all in power and He didn't let Bilaam curse the Jews. Instead, a blessing came out of Bilaam's mouth and the Jews turned it into a song that they still sing to this day!

When the sorcerer Bilaam tried to curse the Jews, God changed the words that came out of his mouth. Those words became a song and a prayer speaking of good morals and spirit: *How good are your tents (your homes), Jacob; and your dwelling places, Israel.*

"The Jews were on a mission—to show the world that there is one true God and that we are supposed to show this by being living examples of unity and by living righteously. "

One Simple Prayer

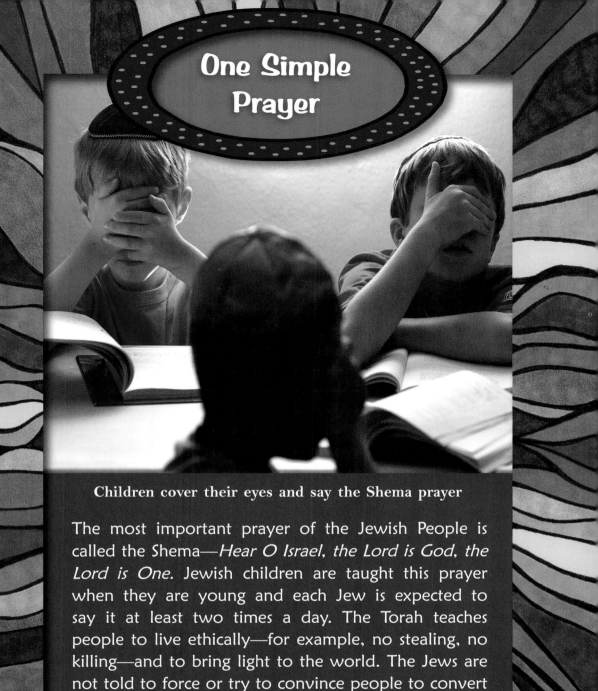

Children cover their eyes and say the Shema prayer

The most important prayer of the Jewish People is called the Shema—*Hear O Israel, the Lord is God, the Lord is One.* Jewish children are taught this prayer when they are young and each Jew is expected to say it at least two times a day. The Torah teaches people to live ethically—for example, no stealing, no killing—and to bring light to the world. The Jews are not told to force or try to convince people to convert to their religion. To them, everyone is a child of God.

Soon Ora would be held high during her Bat Mitzvah

18

Living as a Jew

One day when Danny and I were playing cards, he saw Ora and my mom planning something in the kitchen. "What's happening there?" he asked.

"In a few months, Ora will celebrate her *bat mitzvah*. When a Jewish girl turns twelve years old, it is a special birthday. She now has the responsibility to fulfill the commandments of the Torah as an adult woman. Ora and mother are planning a party, like a birthday party but with a special ritual. They'll make a big batch of bread dough. With a special prayer, Ora will take a small amount of the dough to remember the offerings at the Holy Temple in Jerusalem.

"Can you imagine? Our holy Temple in Jerusalem was destroyed about two thousand years ago, but the Jews still remember it in their prayers and center their worship around it! After Ora says that special blessing—her first time—

the rest of the dough will make the special *challah* bread we eat at the Shabbat meals."

"What about you, Yehuda? Don't you get a party too?" Danny asked.

"Oh, yeah!" I grinned. "A boy steps into his responsibility at age 13. For his *bar mitzvah,* he goes to the synagogue to read from the Torah. So my bar mitzvah will be next year."

Danny grinned with me. "I can't wait for that party!" he said. "Hey, I was talking to my cousin about God and I told him about the things I've seen in your family. But I want to know more details about Jewish laws and other things."

Over our next few visits I shared some more with Danny.

Most people have heard of the Ten Commandments, which came from the Hebrew Bible. They are also known as the Ten Utterances. When Moses came down from Mount Sinai, he brought two stone tablets with these Ten Commandments inscribed in them, five on each stone tablet.

The first four of those are about the Jews' relationship with God. The fifth commandment, honoring and respecting parents, is right next to the commandments about God. It kind of means honoring your parents is next to honoring God. Then the other five of the Ten Commandments teach us how to behave around other people. No murder (that is different from self-defense), no adultery (don't go out with another man's wife), no kidnapping, no lying about what someone else does, and no wanting what your neighbor has.

There are 613 commandments given to the Jews through the Torah. Some of them make sense to us and we can figure out why God would want us to do certain things and not to do other things. Some of the commandments are mysterious. We can't understand God's way of thinking. If we did, we'd be Him!

Out of all the commandments there is no one person who can uphold them all. Some are for men only and some are for women only. Some can only be done in the Land of Israel. Some of the commandments are for service in the Temple in Jerusalem, so no one can do them at present.

Moses and Joshua bow before the Ark in this 1900 painting

King Solomon originally built the Jewish Temple in Jerusalem. In it was the Holy Ark that contained the tablets of the Ten Commandments. The Babylonians eventually destroyed the Temple. The Temple was rebuilt, but then, ancient Rome destroyed the Temple and Jerusalem. For two thousand years, the Jews prayed to return to their land. While there were always some Jews living in the biblical land, today it is known as the modern State of Israel and the majority of Jewish people in the world live there.

Who or What is God?

Sometimes people have the idea that God is an old man who sits on a throne in the clouds. According to Judaism, the Divine has 72 names; each name represents a different aspect of the Infinite. The most well-known name is made up of four letters that Jews do not pronounce. Those four letters arranged in different ways mean: *that which is, that which always was, and that which always will be.* Another way to say it is *"The Eternal."*

Another of God's names is translated as *"The Almighty."* One thing that is often misunderstood is that God is not just masculine. In fact, the feminine aspect of God is called the *Shekhina* (sheh-KHEE-na). To think of God as a man or a woman is to limit something that has no limit.

The Torah teaches that everything that God does is done out of love. God loves and cares about each individual. A human being can never fully understand the world and sometimes it's just plain hard to understand why things are the way they are. And, God has given each person their own power to make this world better, to bring more light, more justice, more goodness, more charity, more love, and more joy.

Jewish Law

Jewish law is called *halacha* (ha-la-KHA), which means "the way." While the basic laws are very clear, it is also made clear that with very few exceptions most of the laws should be broken to save a life. It is against Jewish law to eat certain foods. But if someone would die if he didn't eat, it would actually be a good thing to eat and the food would not be considered forbidden.

Kashrut

The Torah forbids Jews to eat certain foods. All fruits and vegetables are permitted but there are fish, fowl (birds), and animals that are forbidden. The Torah teaches "do not steep a kid in its mother's milk" and so one of the dietary laws forbids eating milk and meat together.

Besides what is permitted or not, there is a special requirement for the *way* that animals for food must be slaughtered. It is done with mercy for the animal. It is swift and clean. The knife must be checked before each and every cut. No animal is ever killed by a machine or a gun. The blood—the life force—of the animal must be returned to the earth.

Prayer

There are two kinds of prayer—formal prayer from a prayer book, and informal prayer, talking to God. According to Judaism, everyone, not just

Jews, can talk to God and have a relationship with Him. There are three parts to prayer:

1. Recognize that you are speaking to the Divine.
2. Ask for something. Yes! Nothing is too small or too big.
3. Say thank you.

Everyone should speak to God in his or her own language. A famous rabbi called Rabbi Nachman said, "You should pour out your heart to God like He is a good friend." While people gather in synagogues to pray, it is also good to pray to God on your own. Rabbi Nachman said it's good to go into nature to pray and talk with God.

Formal prayers are written in Hebrew and translated in many languages. Most of the prayers are thousands of years old. There is a prayer service three times a day. Among the orthodox and Sephardi Jews, a *minyan* (a gathering of ten men, also called a *quorum*) is needed. In the morning, each man wraps *tefilin* on his arms and places it on his head. This is a special ritual that "binds" the men to God. The women are not required to do this ritual.

The home is also a central place to celebrate and pray.

One holiday that centers in the home is Passover. Families gather around a special meal to retell the story of God taking the Jews out of Egyptian slavery.

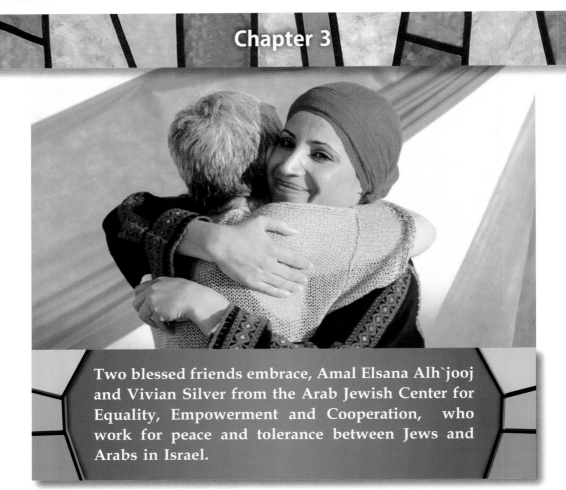

Two blessed friends embrace, Amal Elsana Alh`jooj and Vivian Silver from the Arab Jewish Center for Equality, Empowerment and Cooperation, who work for peace and tolerance between Jews and Arabs in Israel.

Blessings

Besides the prayers, there are blessings that are said over the different kinds of food. There are blessings for seeing lightning or thunder, and even a blessing for seeing an old friend you haven't seen in a long time. These blessings help people be grateful to God and mindful about their everyday lives.

Holy Days (or Holidays)

Most Jewish holidays come from the written Torah. Each week is the Sabbath, and each month is the new moon, a time of renewal. There are three festivals: Pesach (Passover), Shavuot, and Succot. There are other holidays like Hanukkah which came after the written Torah, when the Temple in Jerusalem was reclaimed by the Macabees after it was conquered by the Babylonians.

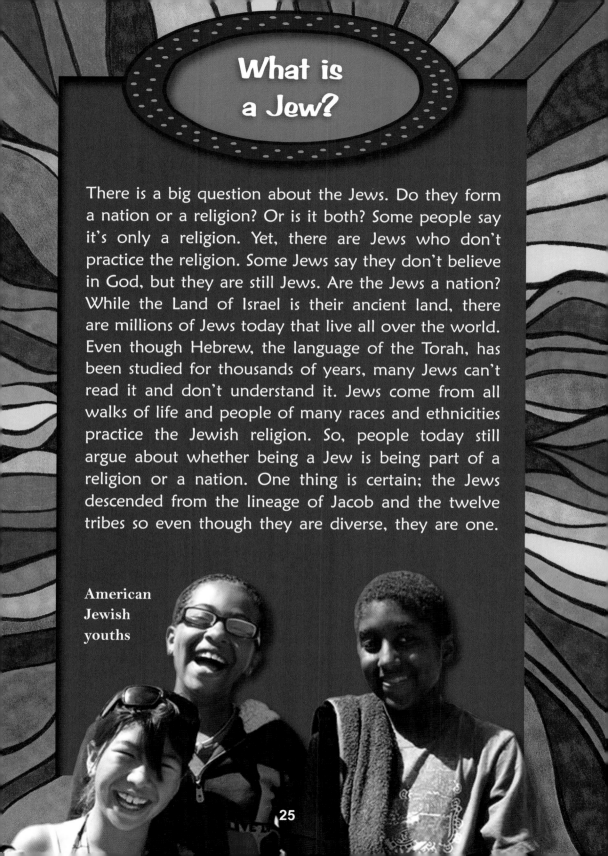

What is a Jew?

There is a big question about the Jews. Do they form a nation or a religion? Or is it both? Some people say it's only a religion. Yet, there are Jews who don't practice the religion. Some Jews say they don't believe in God, but they are still Jews. Are the Jews a nation? While the Land of Israel is their ancient land, there are millions of Jews today that live all over the world. Even though Hebrew, the language of the Torah, has been studied for thousands of years, many Jews can't read it and don't understand it. Jews come from all walks of life and people of many races and ethnicities practice the Jewish religion. So, people today still argue about whether being a Jew is being part of a religion or a nation. One thing is certain; the Jews descended from the lineage of Jacob and the twelve tribes so even though they are diverse, they are one.

American Jewish youths

The Judgment of Solomon by Nicolas Poussin

26

From Generation to Generation

Abraham, Moses, his sister Miriam, and his brother Aaron are all prominent in the Torah and in Jewish history. As the Jewish nation grew, and time passed, other events and stories were recorded by prophets. There were many prophets in ancient times, but there are only a few special teachings that have become part of the body of sacred writings and teachings that are studied and treasured by the Jews.

King Solomon was the Jewish king who built the first holy Temple in Jerusalem. He was known for being the wisest among all men. There are many stories told about his wisdom. One famous story is about two women who came to him with a dispute. They each had a baby and one of them had died. The woman whose baby had died had kidnapped the other woman's baby and said it was hers. They asked the king to pass judgment on the matter. King Solomon said, "Let's cut the baby in half and you can each take a half." The mother of the dead baby agreed that it was a good idea. But the true mother of the baby cried out, "No! Let her take the baby." King Solomon knew who the true mother was. There are many wonderful stories about King Solomon and how wise he was.

The story of **Ruth** is told in the *Scroll of Ruth*. Ruth was a Moabite princess who married a Jew. When her husband died, she left her status of Princess of Moab to follow her mother-in-law, also a widow, back to the Land of Israel to practice Judaism. As a convert, it was not an easy life for

Many artists have been inspired to paint stories from the Hebrew Bible. Here is Julius Schnorr von Carolsfeld's *Ruth in Boaz's Field*, 1828, from the story of Ruth.

Ruth, but it was the only life she wanted. In fact, her story is so treasured that the Jews read it every year in synagogues during the holiday Shavuot in order to remember that everyone standing at Sinai was like a convert—choosing the life of the Torah.

The Scroll of **Esther** records the story of a woman who was a simple Jewess who lived during the time of King Ahasuerus in ancient Persia (modern Iran). The king was looking for a new queen after he ordered the execution of his wife. He held a beauty contest and all the single girls had to be a part of it. Esther did not want any part of it, but she was chosen in the end. Another evil man named Haman advised the king to murder all the Jews and it was Esther—who had not revealed to the king that she herself was a Jew—who stepped forward in her position as queen and exposed the evil Haman. Her courage saved the nation!

The Banquet of Esther and Ahasuerus shows Esther, the wife of King Ahasuerus, telling her husband of the plans his advisor Haman has made to kill the Jewish people.

Rabbi Shimon Bar Yochai is buried in Galilee, in northern Israel. Every year on the anniversary of his death (a holiday called Lag B'Omer), hundreds of thousands of Jews come from all over Israel and the world to visit his grave, to pray, and sing and dance. Called the "Rashbi" for short, he was a figure who taught about the mystical aspects of Judaism.

"This, too, is for the good," taught **Nachum Ish Gam Zu.** Terrible things happened to the man known as Nachum Ish Gam Zu, whose name means *"the man who said 'this, too.'"* No matter what happened to him or anyone else, no matter how hard it was, he taught that life would always turn out for the good.

Sandy Koufax is a famed Jewish baseball player. Besides his outstanding success as a ball player, he made an important decision in 1965. It was the first game of the World Series and the date of that first game fell on the Jewish holy day called Yom Kippur—the holiest of all the Jewish holidays. Koufax made a statement to the world when he stood by his religious beliefs and chose not to play in that important game.

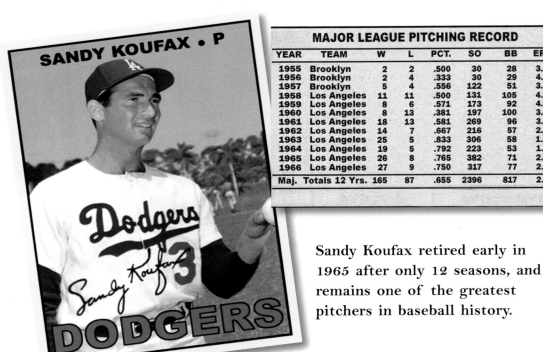

SANDY KOUFAX • P

	MAJOR LEAGUE PITCHING RECORD						
YEAR	TEAM	W	L	PCT.	SO	BB	ERA
1955	Brooklyn	2	2	.500	30	28	3.02
1956	Brooklyn	2	4	.333	30	29	4.91
1957	Brooklyn	5	4	.556	122	51	3.88
1958	Los Angeles	11	11	.500	131	105	4.48
1959	Los Angeles	8	6	.571	173	92	4.05
1960	Los Angeles	8	13	.381	197	100	3.91
1961	Los Angeles	18	13	.581	269	96	3.52
1962	Los Angeles	14	7	.667	216	57	2.54
1963	Los Angeles	25	5	.833	306	58	1.88
1964	Los Angeles	19	5	.792	223	53	1.74
1965	Los Angeles	26	8	.765	382	71	2.04
1966	Los Angeles	27	9	.750	317	77	2.76
Maj. Totals 12 Yrs.		165	87	.655	2396	817	2.76

Sandy Koufax retired early in 1965 after only 12 seasons, and remains one of the greatest pitchers in baseball history.

Rabbi Menachem Mendel Schneerson is a well-known rabbi who was the leader of the Chassidic movement called Chabad. He sent messengers around the world to establish welcome centers for Jews to connect with their roots. Today, there are over 3,300 Chabad centers worldwide!

Rabbi Menachem Mendel Schneerson

There are practicing Jews with all kinds of jobs. Some write TV shows and some are actors. Some are artists or inventors. Many have won special prizes in their fields. Two famous Jewish scientists are **Albert Einstein** whose formulas remain famous and **Jonas Salk** who invented the vaccine for polio.

Albert Einstein   Jonas Salk

Jewish comedian Jon Stewart, standing with Kami the muppet, holds television's top honor, the Peabody Award, for his *Daily Show* on Comedy Central. He wrote and directed *Rosewater*, coming in 2014 , about an innocent political prisoner held in Iran.

Alex Clare and **Matisyahu** are two well-known singers. Your parents might know **Bette Midler** and your grandparents might know **Eddie Fisher. Adam Sandler,** **Natalie Portman,** **Jake Gyllenhaal, Paul Rudd,** and **Mayim Bialik** are popular Jewish actors. **Maurice Sendak** wrote many children's books. Perhaps his most famous is *Where the Wild Things Are.*

What's in a Name?

The Hebrew word for "Jew" is *yehudi* (yeh-hoo-DEE). It comes from the word "grateful." In a way, the name Yehudi means "the grateful one." There is a Hebrew prayer that is said upon waking in the morning that expresses gratitude: *Modeh ani melekh khai v'kaiyam*—I am grateful before You the living and ever-present King, that You returned my soul to me with such kindness. Your faith in me is boundless.

Some examples of names in use today that come from the Hebrew Bible:
Arielle – lion of God
Benjamin – son of my right arm
Daniel – judgment of God
Deborah – honey bee
Hanna – grace
Levi – my heart
Nathaniel – given by God
Ora – light
Ruben – behold (see)! A son.
Sarah – princess

The Biblical name Deborah means honey bee.

LEBANON

SYRIA

GOLAN
HEIGHTS

Haifa

Tiberias

Sea of Galilee

Nazareth

Mediterranean Sea

Netanya

Jenin

Nablus

WEST BANK

Tel Aviv

Ramallah

Ashkelon

Jerusalem ★

Kalia

Bethlehem

Gaza City

Mitzpe Shalem

GAZA

Sderot

Dead Sea

Beersheba

JORDAN

ISRAEL

EGYPT

Areas which came under Israeli control after the 1967 war.

Eilat

Standing as One— Judaism Today

"Come on in Danny," squealed Ora, "Come and meet our aunt. She lives in Israel." Ora and I were sitting at the family computer talking to our Aunt Avia. It was already nighttime in Israel.

"Hi!" said Danny. "It's nice to meet you."

"You, too, I've heard so much about you. Ora and Yehuda have had a lot of fun sharing their lives with you," Aunt Avia smiled warmly.

Danny pulled up a chair, "Wow, it's so cool to be talking to someone from so far away."

"Aunt Avia can tell about Israel if you'd like, Danny."

"Sure, I'd like that," he answered as he pulled a chair closer to the computer.

Aunt Avia enjoyed telling him all about life in the Promised Land and the strength of the Jewish nation.

In 1899 Mark Twain, author of *Huckleberry Finn*, considered one of the greatest of American novelists, wrote an essay about the Jews for *Harper's Magazine* called "Concerning the Jews." In it he wrote: "His contributions to the world's list of great names in literature, science, art, music, finance, medicine, and abstruse [difficult to understand] learning are also way out of proportion to the weakness of his numbers."

She said, "It's logically unexplainable that today the Jewish nation still remains. The Jews make up less than one percent of the world's population. Mark Twain said, '. . . *the Jew ought hardly be heard of, but he is heard of, has always been heard of. He is as prominent on the planet as any other people.'*

"Is it even reasonable after such a long history with so many attempts to wipe out the Jewish nation that they should still be here in the world, and even more astounding is that they cling to their faith that God is in charge, loves mankind, and will bring the prophesies. Many Jews are interested in returning to their roots and are learning the ways of their ancestors."

"It all sounds so meaningful," said Danny.

Aunt Avia continued, "Yes, Danny, it sure is. Each person is rewarded or punished based on who he is. No two people are judged alike. Everyone is given special talents and gifts; and everyone has hardships and challenges too."

Danny wanted to come and hear Aunt Avia again, and over the next few weeks she talked about other Jewish ideas.

Everyone has a chance to help repair the world in the Jewish Faith

Tikkun Olam—Repairing the World

In Judaism, each person is expected to do his or her best to do good in the world. It needs a lot of help and each one of us can have a small part in bringing light into the world. Jewish wisdom teaches that no one is expected to finish the job, but everyone must do his or her part.

The Journey of a Soul

The Jews believe in an afterlife. In fact, Jews are taught that this world we live in is only one of many worlds. The ideas of Heaven and Hell are different for Jews.

Heaven

There isn't really a word for Heaven. The way it's spoken of in Hebrew is *olam haba* which means the "world to come." There is also a notion of *gan eden* which means the Garden of Eden. It is a place of peace and reward and the reward is based on the goodness each person brings into the world with actions like kindness, donations to charity, and learning from the holy books. Perhaps the reward of Heaven is the comfort and pleasure of the good things. For example, what if you helped someone and then in the next world you really got to feel the goodness of that deed?

One way to think of it is kind of like a baby in its mother's womb. The baby grows and grows. It doesn't need eyes in its mother's womb. There isn't a need to taste or to smell. But the baby grows eyes, a nose, lungs, a

Just as a baby in its mother's womb grows body parts it won't need until it is born, the good acts of this world, like giving charity, helping others, honoring your parents, not bullying, not hurting others, or not gossiping are the soul's precious gems to collect and enjoy in the World to Come!

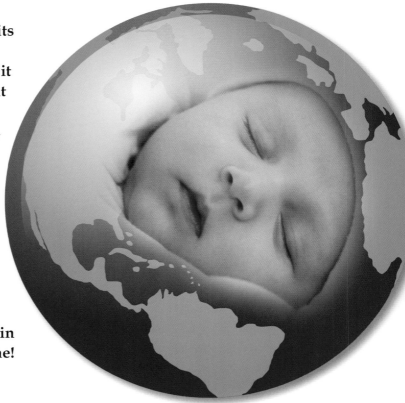

tongue, and all things it will only use in the "next world"—the world of life. So it is with the world to come. Jews believe all the good things a person does in life will make the world to come much sweeter.

Hell

There is not an eternal Hell in Judaism. Though, there are punishments that probably feel like what others might think of as Hell. One way to think of it is like a place of cleaning the soul. The idea of punishment is not so much about your belief but your actions. Just like in life, if you break something, you must fix or replace it. You can say "sorry" but you still have to fix the damage. Cleaning up damage that was done in life doesn't always feel so great, but once the work is done, all feels right again.

The soul has a mission from God and when a person goes off track, it can make the soul not so shiny. One way to think of the Jewish idea of *gehenom* is that it's the place after life where the soul goes for a short time to get clean and bright!

The next year, Danny proudly attended Yehuda's bar mitzvah and met many more members of his friend's family.

True Friends

"You know Yehuda and Ora, I've learned so much about what it means to be a Jew. It hasn't always been easy but it sure is a rich way to live," Danny said.

Ora and I smiled. We both felt so happy that we got to share our beliefs with our friend. "Thanks," we said at the same time.

"I'm glad we get to be friends," I said.

"And I'm also glad your mother is such a great cook!" Danny laughed as we headed to the kitchen for a bite to eat.

One Light

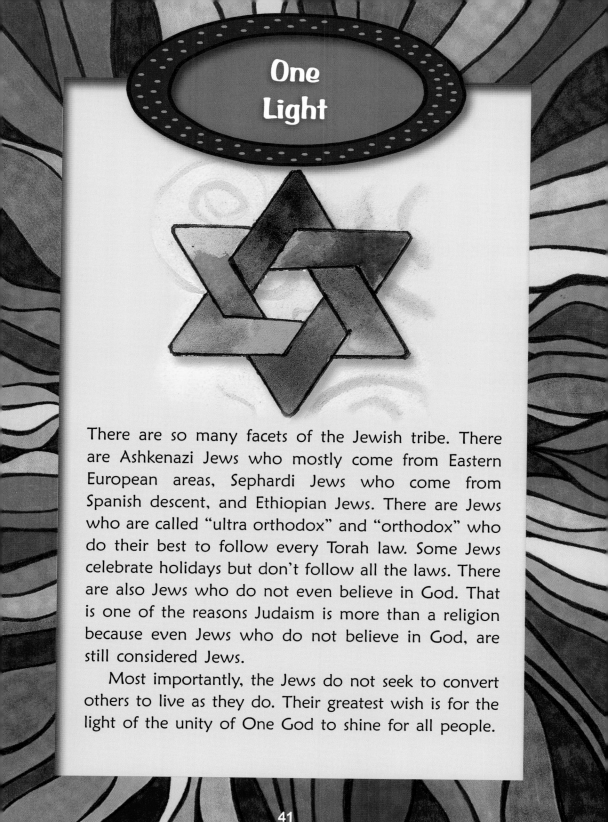

There are so many facets of the Jewish tribe. There are Ashkenazi Jews who mostly come from Eastern European areas, Sephardi Jews who come from Spanish descent, and Ethiopian Jews. There are Jews who are called "ultra orthodox" and "orthodox" who do their best to follow every Torah law. Some Jews celebrate holidays but don't follow all the laws. There are also Jews who do not even believe in God. That is one of the reasons Judaism is more than a religion because even Jews who do not believe in God, are still considered Jews.

Most importantly, the Jews do not seek to convert others to live as they do. Their greatest wish is for the light of the unity of One God to shine for all people.

1812 BCE	Time of Abraham begins
1712 BCE	Time of Isaac begins
1652 BCE	Time of Jacob begins
1428 BCE	Israelites enslaved in Egypt
1392 BCE	Time of Moses begins
1312 BCE	Exodus and Torah given at Mount Sinai
836 BCE	King Solomon begins his rule
422 BCE	Babylonians conquer Israel and destroy temple
352 BCE	Construction of second temple begins
167 BCE	Revolt of Macabees begins
1096	Time of Crusades begins
1348	The Black Plague
1478	The Inquisition begins
1654	First Jews arrive in America
1942	Final Solution created by the Nazis under Adolph Hitler
1948	The State of Israel is declared

Books

Ansh, Tamar. *A Taste of Challah*. Nanuet, New York: Feldheim Publishers, 2007.

Blech, Rabbi Benjamin. *The Complete Idiot's Guide to Understanding Judaism*. 2nd Edition. Royersford, PA: The Alpha Publishing House, 2003.

Blitz, Shmuel. *Bedtime Stories of Jewish Values*. New York: Mesorah Publications Limited, 1998.

DK Eyewitness Books: Judaism. New York: DK Publishing, 2003.

Gross, Judy. *Celebrate: A Book of Jewish Holidays*. New York: Grosset & Dunlap, 2005.

Nestlebaum, Chana. *Positive Word Power for Teens*. New York: Mesorah Publications Limited, 2014.

Schroeder-Hildebrand, Dagmar, and Peter W. Schroeder. *Six Million Paper Clips: The Making of a Children's Holocaust Memorial*. Minneapolis: Kar-Ben Publishing, 2014.

Telushkin, Rabbi Joseph. *The Book of Jewish Values: A Day-by-Day Guide to Ethical Living*. London: Random House, 2011.

An Israel market

Works consulted

Scherman, Nosson. *The Chumash: The Stone Edition,* Full Size (ArtScroll) (English and Hebrew Edition), New York: Mesorah Publications Limited, 1993.

Scherman, Nosson. *The Torah: Haftaros and Five Megillos with a Commentary Anthologized from the Rabbinic Writings,* New York: Mesorah Publications Limited, 1993.

Weissman, Moshe. *The Midrash Says: The Narrative of the Weekly Torah-portion in the Perspective of Our Sages* (Five Vol. Set) New York: Benei Yakov Publications, 1995.

Tel Aviv, Israel

On the Internet

Chabad.org
   http://www.chabad.org/library/article_cdo/aid/36226/jewish/About-Chabad-Lubavitch.htm

Jewish Virtual Library
   http://www.jewishvirtuallibrary.org/jsource/Judaism/jewpop.html

Mark Twain and the Jews
   http://www.simpletoremember.com/jewish/blog/mark-twain-and-the-jews/

Rabbi Ari Khan
   http://www.rabbiarikahn.com/

Simple to Remember
   www.simpletoremember.com

Awe—To be amazed in a way that makes you feel small in all the world.

Bar or Bat mitzvah—The age when a boy (bar) or girl (bat) becomes responsible to observe the commandments as an adult in the nation.

Convert—KON-vert—Someone who joins another religion that he or she was not born into.

Eternal—ee-TUR-nul—For all time (above and beyond time), also a name that people can use to describe God as in "The Eternal."

Famine—FAH-min—A period of time when there is very little or no food to eat.

Halakha—The body of Jewish law, from the root word meaning "the way."

Idolatry—eye-DOLL-uh-tree—To worhip idols in a religious way.

Jew—A person who is born to a Jewish mother or who converts, from the Hebrew root word for thankful.

Oppressed—When a group is held back from living freely and flourishing.

Plagues—PLAYGS—Events that cause much death or destruction.

Prophet—A person who serves as a voice for God or a deity, or through divine inspiration.

Ravaged—RAH-vijd—Destroyed.

Revelation—rev-ah-LAY-shun—When something is revealed.

Rituals—rich-CHEW-alls—Actions done regularly that have a special or spiritual meaning or significance.

Ruler—Leader who was not elected but is in charge by military take over or birth right.

Sacred—SAY-krid—Holy and deep spiritual meaning.

Shekhina—The feminine aspect of God.

Tribe—A group of people who are set apart socially.

Widow—WIH-doe—A woman whose husband died and who is living unmarried.

Index

Abraham   12, 13, 16, 27

Bar mitzvah   20, 40

Bat mitzvah   18, 19

Blessing   7, 8, 16, 19, 24
    Of the children   8

Calendar, Jewish   9

Clare, Alex   32

Egypt (see slavery)

Einstein, Albert   30

Esther   29

God   7, 8, 13, 15, 16, 25, 36, 46
    commandments   20
    in prayer   17
    revelation of   11, 12
    talks to Moses   13
    what is God?   21–22

Heaven   15, 37, 38

Hebrew song   6

Hell   37, 39

Hillel   6

Holidays   8, 24
    Lag b'Omer   30
    Passover   14, 15, 23
    Purim   29
    Shavuot   11, 29

Israel   13, 20, 21, 24, 25, 28, 30, 35

Jerusalem   19, 20, 21, 24, 27

Jew   25, 41, 46

Kashrut/Kosher   15, 22

Koufax, Sandy   30

Law, Jewish   7, 15, 17, 20, 22, 41

Moses   11, 14, 21, 27

Names, meanings   33

Nimrod   13

Prayer   7, 17, 19, 22–23, 24, 33

Repairing the world   37

Ruth   28

Sabbath, Shabbat   7, 8, 9, 20, 24

Salk, Jonas   30

Schneerson, Menachem Mendel   30

Sendak, Maurice   32

Sinai (Mount)   11, 12, 15, 16, 20, 29

Slavery in Egypt
    Story of Exodus   11–15

Solomon, King   21

Sorcerer (Bilaam)   16

Soul   12, 33, 37, 39

Stewart, Jon   32

Ten Commandments   12, 15, 19, 20, 21

Twain, Mark   36

World War II   5

Laya Saul grew up in Los Angeles, California. She went to Hebrew school as a young girl and celebrated the Jewish holidays growing up. Now that she has a family of her own, she delights in celebrating the cycle of Jewish holidays. Lighting one candle can chase away a lot of darkness and Laya believes that each person is a candle that brings light into the world. She has written other books including her book for teens called *You Don't Have to Learn Everything the Hard Way* that is a guide to maturing. Today, she lives in Israel with her family, their dog, cat, and five backyard hens!